Zoroastrianism and the Teachings
of Zarathustra:
The Zoroastrian Creed and
Selected Sacred Hymns
of Zoroaster with Prayers and
Liturgies of the Faith
in Modern-Day English

Zoroastrianism and the Teachings of Zarathustra: The Zoroastrian Creed and Selected Sacred Hymns of Zoroaster with Prayers and Liturgies of the Faith in Modern-Day English

Translated by L.H. Mills and James Darmesteter, *Sacred Books of the Middle East*, American Edition (1898) and James Hope Moulton, *Early Zoroastrianism*, London (1913)

Edited by Anahita Azad (2021)

ISBN: 9798-451233955

TABLE OF CONTENTS

"The thought manifests the word;

The word manifests the deed;

The deed develops into habit;

And habit hardens into character;

So watch the thought and its ways with care,

And let them spring forth from love

Born out of compassion for all beings.

As the shadow follows the body,

as we think, so we become."

(Source unknown)

An Introduction to Zoroastrianism

Referred to as Mazdayasna by its followers, Zoroastrianism is widely regarded as the world's first monotheistic religion, meaning that it worships a single divine god. The Zoroastrian faith was founded by the prophet Zarathustra in Persia somewhere around 1200 BC. Known to the Greeks as Zoroaster, the prophet believed that God had entrusted him with a message for all humankind, and he preached this message in plain words to ordinary people living during his time. His teachings were originally handed down orally from generation to generation, but later were written in in Middle Persian some time during the third Iranian Empire.

During the Persian empires, from 559 BC to 651 AD, Zoroastrianism was the dominant world religion. Zoroastrians believe that the soul is immortal and that it will be judged immediately after death. Based upon this concept of the immortality of the soul, the faith emphasizes the worship of wisdom and truth by striving for good thoughts, good words, and good deeds. These teachings were radical for their time because of their emphasis on human choice and human thought as powerful forces in the universe. With a foundation on these tenets, it is not surprising that the teachings of

Zoroastrianism have had a major influence on other world religions, and the faith is still practiced around the world today, especially in Iran, India, and North America.

The supreme being or God in the Zoroastrian faith is called Ahura Mazda. Ahura Mazda created the world and all good things, including people. The Holy Spirit of Ahura Mazda is called the Spenta Mainyu or the Good Spirit. Opposing the Spenta Mainyu, the Anghra Mainyu is the Destructive Spirit, who is the creator of all evil things and the very embodiment of evil.

There are six manifestations of Ahura Mazda called the Amesha Spentas, which are sometimes referred to as the Immortal Souls or Bountiful Immortals, each of which represents one aspect of creation. The word "spenta" denotes holiness and sanctity, and therefore these manifestations are positive creative forces in the universe.

One of the Amesha Spentas is Vohu Manah, sometimes referred to as Vohu Manu or Vohu Manoh, which supports the concepts of Good Purpose, Good Thought, and Good Mind. This correct, positive state of mind empowers individuals to carry out their duties of good thoughts, good words, and good deeds as they interact with the world around them. Spenta Armaiti, referred to as Beneficent Devotion in the texts in this book, is the spirit of faith and devotion and another of the Amesha Spentas. This deity presides over the earth and guides and protects believers.

There are a number of other divine and evils beings in the Zoroastrian faith. This book provides information about each one as they are mentioned in the text. To give a brief introduction here, the Daevas are evil spirits with disagreeable and unpleasant characteristics. These false gods or demons can corrupt the spirit, and accordingly, they are to be avoided at all costs. The Druj, which refers to the concept of dishonesty, lies, and deceit, is another evil force.

The Druj is opposed to Asha, the divine word of truth and righteousness. The Zoroastrian faith is perhaps best summed up by the phrase: "Good thoughts; Good words; Good deeds," so one must strive to think good thoughts of themselves, others, and the word around them. These good thoughts will then lead to good speech and ultimately to good deeds or actions. This concept is essentially the core of the Zoroastrian faith.

Cleanliness is other core concept in the faith, and "the clean" is often mentioned throughout

Zoroastrian worship. Referring to purity and sanctity, the clean is linked to both personal and communal aspects of worship, which are regulated in the faith's rites and rituals in order to protect the believer from impurities or other forces that could pollute the mind and soul.

The main scripture of the faith is known as the *Avesta*. The main parts of the scripture are the Yasna, including the sacred liturgy and hymns of Zarathustra, the Khorda Avesta or Book of Common Prayer, the Visperad, which includes other hymns, prayers, and litanies, and the Vendidad, which is used for religious observances. The Yasna contains two very important types of texts for the faith: the Gathas and the Creed. The Gathas are the divine words and songs uttered by the prophet Zarathustra, which are the sacred hymns of the faith. The Yasna also contains the Zoroastrian creed or declaration of the faith in chapter 12.

Sraosha, which means Obedience, is the divine messenger of the God Ahura Mazda. The word "sraosha" in Middle Persian means to hear or listen attentively, so this divinity embodies the divine word of Ahura Mazda and signifies humankind's obedient and attentive listening to the divine word.

Representing Asha, or the holy light of God, fire is a central sacred symbol in the faith. The major Zoroastrian temples have consecrated fires burning perpetually in them and members of the faith will often pray in front of a fire.

This book will first provide the Zoroastrian Creed, or declaration of faith, followed by selected hymns, prayers, and liturgies of the faith. All of the selections are written in modern-day, easy-to-understand English.

YASNA 12

THE ZOROASTRIAN CREED

1. I curse the evil forces that we call the Daevas. I worship Mazda. I support Zarathustra, who is hostile to the evil forces, loves Ahura's teachings, and praises and worships the six divine beings called the Amesha Spentas. I accredit all good things to Ahura Mazda, whose is Asha, the holy light of sacred order and truth, and whose is the light. May Ahura's light shine on us all.

2. I choose the good Spenta Armaiti of Beneficent Devotion for myself; let it be mine.

I renounce theft and robbery and all other crimes.

3. I desire freedom of movement and freedom of accommodation for all those who dwell upon this earth. With reverence for Asha, the holy light of sacred order and truth, I willingly make an offering and vow that I shall do nothing to damage the Mazdayasnian faith or its followers.

4. I reject the authority of the evil forces called the Daevas, the most offensive and the most damaging of beings. I reject the followers of evil and anyone who harms humanity. I reject

11

them in my thoughts, speech, and actions. I reject them publicly.

5. As Ahura Mazda taught Zarathustra during their meeting, conversations, and discussions;

6. Just as Zarathustra rejected all evil, I, too, also reject all evil as Mazda-worshipper and supporter of Zarathustra.

7. As the belief of the waters, the belief of the plants, the belief of the well-made creation; as the belief of Zarathustra, fulfilling destiny and endowed with Asha, the holy light of sacred order and truth, so too I worship Mazda in these beliefs and teachings.

8. I affirm that I am a Mazda-worshipper, a Zoroastrian, having vowed it and professed it. I commit my mind to well-thought thought; I commit my speech to the well-spoken word; I commit my life to well-done deeds.

9. I pledge myself to the Mazdayasnian religion, which lessens the hurt and pain in the world, which is endowed with Asha, Ahura's holy light; which is and shall be the greatest, best, and most beautiful of all religions. I ascribe all good to Ahura Mazda. This is the creed of the Mazdayasnian religion.

Sacred Liturgy and Hymns of

Zarathustra

Ahunavaiti Gatha

YASNA 28

1. With outspread hands in petition for Your help, O Mazda, the Right, I will pray for the works of Your holy spirit, that I may please the will of Good Thought.

2. I will serve you, Mazda Ahura! Give us Good Thought through truth and righteousness with the blessings of the earthly and divine, and the physical and spiritual, which bring the faithful joy.

3. I will praise you like never before, Right and Good Thought and Mazda Ahura, and for those who eternally grow and rule in Piety; hear my prayer and come to me.

4. I have set my heart on watching over the soul, in union with Good Thought, knowing the rewards of Mazda Ahura for our good works. And I will, while I have power and strength, teach all people to seek what is Right.

5. O Asha, I see Good Thought and You, who knows me. I see the throne of the mightiest Ahura and the followers of

Mazda. With this vow on our lips, we will overturn evil, for you, the Greatest.

6. Now grant long-enduring, powerful help as a gift to Zarathustra, O Mazda, with Good Thought, given through that truth and righteousness which we call Asha, according to your true words. And to us, O Ahura, grant us help to overcome the hatred of our enemies.

7. Grant the reward of the blessing of Good Thought, O Ahura! O Piety, give our desire to Vishtaspa, our holy patron, and to me as well, O Mazda our Ruler,

and grant that your Prophet may be
heard.

8. The best I ask of You, for the heroes
and for those others to whom You would
offer it, is the best gift of Good Mind
through all time, O Lord, Ahura, of one
will with Asha, the holy light of sacred
order and truth.

9. With these blessings, O Ahura, may
we never cause you displeasure, we who
have been so eager to bring you songs of
praise. You are the mightiest to incite
love and the Dominion of Blessings, O
Mazda and Right and Best Thought.

10. You know the wise as worthy for their good deeds and their good thought. Fulfill their longing for all that they hope to attain. I ask this because I know that you will hear and answer my words of prayer.

11. I will preserve Right and Good Thought forevermore. Instruct me so that I may teach others, O Mazda Ahura, from Your spirit and by Your mouth, how it shall be from the beginning.

YASNA 30

1. Now I will proclaim to those who will hear the things that the understanding person should remember, for hymns unto Ahura and prayers to Good Thought; also the joy that is with the heavenly lights, which through Right shall be seen by those who think wisely.

2. Hear the best things with your ears, and look upon these things with clear-seeing thought, because you must decide between the two Beliefs of good and evil. Indeed, each person must decide which path to take before they complete their

time on earth, always considering which thoughts, words, and actions are pleasing to You, O Ahura!

3. Now the two primordial Spirits, who have revealed themselves in visions as Twins, are the Better and the Bad in thought and word and action. The wise person correctly chooses the Better, but the foolish person does not.

4. And when these two Spirits, the Better and the Bad, came together in the beginning, they created Life and Not-Life, and the followers of the Lie shall live in the Worst Existence, but the Best

Existence shall be lived by those who follow the Right.

5. Of these twin Spirits, those that follow the Lie chose doing the worst things, while the holiest Spirits chose the Right. And the Right clothes us with heavenly garments. So likewise, we are eager to please Ahura Mazda with our dutiful actions.

6. When confronted with choosing between the Better and the Bad, the evil spirits that we call the Daevas chose the Bad, and they drew more closely to the Bad as they shared company together,

and they chose the Worst Thought. Then they rushed together to Violence in order to harm all of humanity.

7. Then Dominion came to humanity, and Good Mind, and Right and Piety gave us life and strength, and by Your judgement we will be fortified and emboldened and gain the prize over the others.

8. So when the time comes for sins to be punished, O Mazda, at Your command, Good Thought will establish the Dominion throughout our existence on earth, and You shall rightly judge those who lie and commit wrongdoings.

9. Let us make this world advance, O Mazda and all the Ahuras; come to us, and grant us admission into your company and that truth and righteousness that we call Asha, so that we may collect our thoughts even when our reason is shaky.

10. Truly I say to you, those who lie shall destroy their joy in this life, but those who earn a good reputation will take part in the promised reward in the fair dwelling place of Good Thought, of Mazda, and of Right.

11. If all human beings would mark these commandments which Mazda has ordained — of happiness and pain, of the long punishment for the followers of the evil force that we call the Druj, and of blessings for the followers of the Right — then hereafter all shall be well.

YASNA 31

1. So, being mindful of your commands, we will proclaim words unpleasant for the evil ones to hear when the actions of lies and deception have destroyed the creatures of Right. But these words shall be most welcome to those that give their hearts to Mazda.

2. And when there are times that it is difficult to see or know the better path, or it is not in sight, then will Ahura Mazda will come to our aid to help us judge between good and evil, both of whom

Ahura knows very well, that we may live according to the Right.

3. Please tell me, O Mazda, what award You give through Your Holy Spirit and through the holy light of the Fire, and You have shown the followers of good and evil which decision is for the wise. Tell me so that I may know and be emboldened through my own speech to bring all of humanity to know You.

4. If the righteousness and wisdom that we call Asha is to be brought to us and Mazda and the Deities, please also bring to us the Good Mind that we call Vohu

Manah, so that we might vanquish the Lie.

5. Please tell me that You, O the Right, will help me find and determine good choices and to keep in mind the Good Thought. Indeed, with these good choices others may envy me. Tell me of all these things, O Mazda Ahura, that shall or shall not be.

6. I know Right's truthful word of Welfare and of Immortality because they speak to me. Let all good things come to me, and

let the Dominion of Mazda continue, and let Good Thought prosper within me.

7. And those that by wisdom created Right thought, "let the blessed realms be filled with Light." You exalt the realms that the Best Thought possesses, O Mazda, through Your Spirit, which is ever constant, O Ahura.

8. I recognize You, O Mazda, in my thought, that You are the First and the Last — that the good mind that we call Vohu Manah is Your child. I understand You through the vision which You have granted me, that You are the true Creator

of the Righteousness and Truth of Asha, and that You are the ruler who judges the actions of our lives.

9. Beneficent Devotion, Creation, and the Wisdom of the Spirit are Yours, O Mazda Ahura, because you gave even the lowliest creatures the choice about the manner of their own procreation.

10. So Beneficent Devotion, called Spenta Armaiti, chose the ruler of the raising and management of animals to guard the Right and those that advance Good Thought. Those that have no knowledge in the raising and

management of animals, O Mazda, however eager they may be, have no part in this good message.

11. O Mazda, in the beginning You created the Individual and Individuality through Your Spirit, and granted us powers of understanding when you made life within our bodies. And you created teachings and actions which allow us to exercise our convictions with free will.

12. Then those that know and those that do not know the Right, each according to their own heart and mind, will speak with truth or will speak the words of the Lie.

And overseeing both the Truth and the Lie, Spenta Armaiti, who is Beneficent Devotion, will grant the spirit to those that are wavering.

13. And you, O Ahura, through the truth and righteousness of Asha, are aware of both our public and secret acts, and you have the power to punish our wrongdoings and to decide how severe that punishment should be. You are observing all of this through Asha with sharp vision in Your eyes.

14. So I come to ask You, O Ahura, how will these things will happen: the

31

consequences that are recorded for the righteous, as well as the consequences that shall be assigned to the followers of the evil that we call the Druj. I am asking You how these things shall be when they come to Your judgment.

15. And I also ask You what repercussions will come to those who seek to exalt liars and those who commit ill deeds, as well as those who maliciously harm animals and their keepers, even though the keepers bring no harm to them.

16. And I ask, too, whether the understanding person, who strives to advance Your Dominion over the house, land, and community through Asha, will become more like You, O Mazda Ahura. How will these understanding people be and how will they act?

17. Which is the greater: the beliefs of followers of that truth and righteousness which we call Asha or the beliefs of the followers of that evil which we call the Druj? Let those that know inform the wise, and no longer let those that know

nothing deceive others. Be the Teacher of Good Thought to us, O Mazda Ahura.

18. Let none of you listen to the words and commands of the followers of the Druj, for they bring house and family and community into misery and destruction. Resist them powerfully!

19. We must listen to those who have understood Asha, to the wise Healer of Life, O Ahura, who can demonstrate that there is truth in their words. For when the truth of the words of our mouths pass through Your red Fire, O Mazda, you will

assign consequences to evil-doers and

rewards to those who seek the Good.

20. Because those who come over to

Righteous shall in the future be far off

from the long age of misery and

darkness, of ill food, and crying of sorrow.

And those who follow the Lie shall be

cast into this misery and darkness as a

consequence of their own actions.

21. By virtue of His absolute rule, Mazda

Ahura will grant eternal communion with

Wholeness and Immortality, with Asha,

with desirable Dominion, and with that

good mind that we call Vohu Manah, to

those that in spirit and in action are his
friends.

22. All of these things are clear to those
of understanding, who have realized
them with their thoughts, who uphold
Asha together with good Dominion by
their words and deeds. Those of
understanding, O Mazda Ahura, shall be
the most invaluable helpers to You.

YASNA 34

1. We pray that you might grant us
multitudes of Immortality and Right, and
Dominion of Welfare for the actions, the
words, and our worship of You, O Mazda.

2. And set in Your outer court, adorned
with hymns of praise, those souls who
follow the Right with their actions of the
good spirit that we call Spenta Mainyu.

3. We will make sacrifices, offerings,
worship, and service to You and to the
Truth and Righteousness of Asha, so that
You may bring all creatures to perfection
through Good Thought in Your

established Dominion, because the reward of the wise is forever secure with You, O Mazda.

4. And may Your Fire, which is mighty through Right, O Ahura, promised and powerful, manifest delight for the faithful, but visible torment for the enemy, according to Your judgment.

5. I ask You, O Mazda, do You have Dominion and power, Right and Good Thought, to do as I pray, to protect your poor people, we who have renounced the wrong-doers and those who follow evil?

6. If all these things are true, O Mazda, Right and Good Thought, then I ask that You would reverse any ill fortune that befalls me as Your gift, that I may come before you again more joyfully with worship and praise.

7. Can those who by their doctrines turn the known inheritance of Good Thought into misery and sorrow ever be true to You, O Mazda? I know none other than You, O Right, so I pray that you would protect us.

8. These creators of misery and sorrow, through hatred of Your commandments,

cause us to be afraid, O Mazda, and fear is especially dangerous for those who are weak. They will not have the Right in their thought, and the Good Abode shall be far from them.

9. These people of evil action, who shun the holy Piety, which is so precious to Your wise ones, O Mazda, have no part in Good Thought, and the Right shrinks back far from them, just as wild beasts shrink from us.

10. Those of understanding and good will have instructed people to cling to the action of the Good Thought that we call

Vohu Manah, and to the Holy Piety that we call Spenta Armaiti, the creator and comrade of Right. Wise and hopeful are all those that are in Your Dominion, O Ahura.

11. And You will grant us gifts for sustenance, even as food at a banquet feast. Piety linked with Right shall advance the Dominion of Good Thought, and its permanence and power. By these, O Mazda, you bless the enemies of your enemies.

12. What is Your direction for us? And what are Your intentions for us? What of

praise and worship? Proclaim these things, O Mazda, that we may hear the direction that Destiny will assign to us. By Your Right, teach us the paths of Good Thought in which the blessed walk.

13. The divine insight of the future benefactors will be granted as a reward that was prepared for the wise – a reward which You will determine, O Mazda – even that way of Good Thought, O Ahura, which You spoke about to me, on a way well made by Right.

14. Then, O Mazda, You will give the precious reward by the action of Good

Thought to the bodily life of those who are in the community, the promise of your good doctrine, O Ahura, that of the wisdom which exalts communities through Right.

15. O Mazda, make known to me the best teachings and actions, of which Good Thought and the Right are worthy of praise. Through your Dominion, O Ahura, assure us that humankind shall be capable of these things, according to Your will.

YASNA 35

PRAYER FOR THE PRACTICE AND PROPAGATION OF THE FAITH

1. We sacrifice to Ahura Mazda, the holy ruler, and to the Bountiful Immortals with their immortal souls and guardian spirits, who rightly have power over all things; and we sacrifice to the entire creation of the clean, the spiritual and the earthly, with the earnest blessing of the beneficial ritual, with the earnest blessing of the gracious Religion, the Mazdayasnian Faith.

2. We praise good thoughts, good words, and good deeds, in the present and in the future.

We give them homage and respect, and we do this more and more because we praise the good from which they emanate.

3. Therefore, O Ahura Mazda, Blessed Righteous, we choose to think, speak, and perform those good thoughts, words, and deeds, among true good thoughts, words, and deeds, which are the best for both the earthly and divine; and together with these greatest gifts and best actions, we pray for Kine, the pure creation, that all creation may have comfort and sustenance from both the famous and the unknown, from both the powerful and the weak.

5. The Kingdom truly belongs to the best of the good rulers, because we attribute and relinquish it to Mazda, and we give all possession of it to Mazda Ahura and to Righteousness.

6. Thus, all of humanity completely and genuinely knows Mazda and Righteousness, so let them declare their faith, carry it out in their daily lives, and educate others about it.

7. We respect and cherish Your sacrifice and give you praise, O Ahura Mazda! And we will be mindful of the nurture of all creation. Therefore, let us impart and declare our faith for You as You see fit for us to do.

8. Under your care and with the protection afforded by sacred rituals, let us actively fulfill Your teachings toward each and every one of the creatures which live with us as a gift from both the divine and temporal worlds.

9. In these words, O Ahura Mazda! we proclaim Righteousness, and with a clear mind, we acknowledge You as the one who both supports us in our proclamation and who casts light upon all creation as it is.

10. And because of Your Righteousness, Your Good Mind, and Your Sovereign Power, and with the purpose of our praises of You, O Ahura Mazda! and for further praises still, by

Your spoken word, and for even further

spoken words, through worship of You, and

for even more worship, we thus proclaim

them, and ask You to grant us light.

YASNA 36

TO AHURA AND THE FIRE

1. We approach You, O Ahura and the Fire,
the primeval ones in Your holy house, O
Ahura Mazda, Your most abundant Spirit! And
to those who would defile your holy flame,
You will defile them in turn.

2. Grant us eternal devotion, O Fire of the
Lord, and come to us, with the loving, familiar
blessing, with the praise of highest adoration.
Come to assist us in this our greatest
undertaking of the efforts of our devotion.

3. You are truly the Fire of Ahura Mazda; the most abundant Spirit. Therefore, Yours is the most powerful of all names for grace, O Holy Fire of the Lord!

4. And therefore we come to You, O Ahura, with the help of Your Good Mind, which You have generously granted to us, with Your Righteousness, and with the speech and actions imparted by Your good wisdom.

5. Therefore, we bow before You, and we direct our prayers to You with confessions of our guilt, O Ahura Mazda, with all the good thoughts, which You alone do inspire in us,

with all the well-spoken words, and well-done deeds, with these we come to You.

6. And to Your most beauteous body, we make our deep acknowledgments, O Ahura Mazda, to those stars which are Your body; and to that one, the highest of the high, which we call the Sun.

YASNA 37

TO AHURA, THE HOLY CREATION, THE GUARDIAN SPIRITS OF THE JUST, AND THE BOUNTIFUL IMMORTALS

1. Thus, we worship Ahura Mazda, who made all living creation, and Righteousness, which comes to life in that which is clean, and the waters, and the wholesome plants, the stars, and the earth, and all existing beings and objects that are good.

2. We worship Ahura, and Ahura's benevolent Sovereign Power and greatness, and the preeminent wind and atmosphere which abide

with all creation and care for its protection and support.

3. And we worship Ahura, our ruler, dear Mazda, the most benevolent of names. We worship Mazda with our bones, with our flesh, with our bodies and our lives. We worship Mazda to the very core of our beings. And we worship the Fravashis, the Guardian Spirits of the saints and of all holy people.

4. And we worship Righteousness, which is the best, the most beautiful and generous spirit which is endowed with light in all good things.

5. And we worship the Good Mind of Ahura, and Mazda's Sovereign Power, and the Good Faith, the good law of our prudence, and Piety, the ready mind within Your people.

YASNA 38

TO THE EARTH AND THE SACRED WATERS

1. Now we worship this earth which bears us, together the Amesha Spentas who govern all of creation, O Ahura Mazda, those Spentas that we worship in admiration of their sanctity.

2. We make sacrifices to their devotion, their capabilities, their inquiries of duty, and their wise acts of holy reverence, and their sanctity, their strength, fame, and wealth.

3. O waters! Now we worship you, you that shower upon us from above, and as well as those waters that stand in pools and vessels,

and those that spring forth. Of Ahura, you that serve us all in helpful ways, when shallow and when full-flowing, and effective for healthful bathing, we seek you for both the divine and the temporal.

4. For these reasons, Ahura Mazda gave you names, O beneficent waters, when Ahura who made all good things created you. And we worship you by these names, and we become charmed by you, and we bow before you, and direct our prayers to you with full acknowledgment of our debt to you. O waters, you are productive, and you are parental. With your warmth, you nourish the frail and needy. The waters which have once been

rulers of us all, we acknowledge you as the

best, and the most beautiful. All this is yours:

the goodness you contribute, reaching us in

our sickness or misfortune, supporting our life!

YASNA 39

TO THE KINE, THE SOUL OF ALL CREATION

1. And now we sacrifice to the Kine, the soul of all creation. To this created body, we make sacrifices and offerings to the souls of all living beings.

2. And we worship all beings, both tame and wild, and the souls of the saints wherever they were born, of all genders, whose good consciences are winning the battle against evil, and will conquer or have conquered evil.

3. And now we worship the Bountiful Immortal Souls of all genders. We worship them, ever

living and ever helpful, who dwell beside the holy.

4. As You, O Ahura Mazda, have thought and spoken, as you have determined, and done these things to bring about that which is good, therefore we make offerings to You, and praise and worship You, and bow down before You, and pray to You, Ahura, and make confessions of our sins.

5. Thus, we come to You with our family, with that of blessed Righteousness, and the Good Faith, the law of our prudence, and Piety, the ready mind within Your people.

YASNA 44

1. This I ask You, tell me truly, Ahura, as to prayer, how it should be to You. O Mazda Ahura, might one like You teach to a friend such as I am, and through kindly Right give us support, that Good Thought may come to us.

2. This I ask You, tell me truly, Ahura, whether atonement shall bring blessedness to those that meet with them at the beginning of the Best Existence. Surely he, O Right, the holy one, who watches in his spirit the transgressions of all, if himself the benefactor of all that lives.

3. This I ask You, tell me truly, Ahura. Who is the Father of Right? Who determined the path of sun and stars? Who is it by whom the moon waxes and wanes again? This, O Mazda, and yet more, I am eager to know.

4. This I ask You, tell me truly, Ahura. Who upholds the earth beneath and the heavens from falling? Who tends to the waters and the plants? Who gave swiftness to winds and clouds? Who is, O Mazda, creator of Good Thought?

5. This I ask You, tell me truly, Ahura. What artist made light and darkness? What artist made sleep and waking? Who made morning,

noon, and night, that call the understanding to their duty?

6. This I ask You, tell me truly, Ahura, whether what I proclaim is indeed the truth. Will Right with its actions give aid? Will Piety? Will Good Thought announce itself from the Dominion?

7. This I ask You, tell me truly, Ahura. Who created together with Dominion the precious Piety? Who made by wisdom the child obedient to the parent? I strive to recognize by these things You, O Mazda, creator of all things through the holy spirit.

8. This I ask You, tell me truly, Ahura. I could keep in mind your design, O Mazda, and

understand correctly the maxims of life which I ask of Good Thought and Right. How will my soul partake of the good that brings growth and well-being?

9. This I ask You, tell me truly, Ahura, whether for the Self that I would bring to perfection, that of the one of insight, the Lord of Dominion would make promises of the sure Dominion, one of your likenesses, O Mazda, who dwells in one abode with Right and Good Thought?

10. This I ask You, tell me truly, Ahura. The Religion which is best for all that are, which in union with Right should prosper all that is mine, will they duly observe it, the religion of my

creed, with words and action of Piety, in desire for your good things, O Mazda?

11. This I ask You, tell me truly, Ahura, whether Piety will extend to those to whom your Religion shall be proclaimed? I was ordained at the first for this by You; all others I look upon with hatred of spirit.

12. This I ask You, tell me truly, Ahura. Who among those with whom I would speak is righteous, and who is a liar? On which side is the enemy? Or are they the enemies, the Liars who oppose your blessings? How shall it be with them? Are they not to be thought of as an enemy?

13. This I ask You, tell me truly, Ahura, whether we shall drive the Lie away from us to those who being full of disobedience will not strive after fellowship with Right, nor trouble themselves with counsel of Good Thought.

14. This I ask You, tell me truly, Ahura, whether I would put the Lie into the hands of Right, to cast it down by your words, to bring about a destruction among the Liars, to bring torment and enmity upon them, O Mazda.

15. This I ask You, tell me truly, Ahura, if you have power over this to ward off from me through Right, when the two opposing hosts of good and evil meet in battle according to those

decrees which you will firmly establish. Which of the two will You give victory?

16. This I ask You, tell me truly, Ahura. Who is victorious to protect by your doctrine of all that exist? By vision, assure me how to set up the judge that heals the world. Then let them have Obedience coming with Good Thought unto every person that You desire, O Mazda.

17. This I ask You, tell me truly, Ahura, whether through you I shall attain my goal, O Mazda, even attachment unto you, and that my voice may be effectual, that Welfare and Immortality may be ready to unite according to that promise with those who join themselves with Right.

18. This I ask You, tell me truly, Ahura, whether I shall indeed, O Right, earn the reward, even an extravagant one, which was promised to me, O Mazda, as well as through You, the future gift of Welfare and Immortality.

19. This I ask You, tell me truly, Ahura. He that will not give the reward to those that earn it, even to the people who fulfilling their promises by performing what they have undertaken. What penalty shall come to those who do not fulfil their promises at the present? I know that which shall come to them in the end.

20. This I ask You, tell me truly, Ahura. Have the Daevas ever exercised good dominion? And I ask of those who see how for the

Daevas' sake animals were brought to violence, instead of being taken care of in the pastures that prosper through Right.

YASNA 52

A PRAYER FOR SANCTITY AND ITS

BENEFITS

1. I pray with blessings for benefits, and for the good, even for the entire creation of the holy; I pray for these things for that which exists now, for that which is just coming into life, and for that which shall exist eternally. I pray for the sanctity that grants us prosperity, which provides us with shelter, which goes on hand in hand with sanctity, which joins with it, and becomes its close companion as it delivers forth its teachings.

2. Sanctity bears every form of healing virtue which comes to us in waters, in plants, and in

other living beings, and defeats the harmful malice of evil and the servants of evil who might harm this dwelling and those who abide here.

3. Sanctity bears forth all good gifts, and better blessings, both those offered early and later, leading to successes, and for a providing us with abiding shelter. And so, the greatest, the best, and most beautiful benefits of sanctity fall likewise to us.

4. For the sacrifice, adoration, redemption, and the praise of the Bountiful Immortal Souls, for bringing prosperity to this house, and for the prosperity of the entire creation of the holy and the clean, and likewise for the opposition of all

evil creation, I pray now as I praise through

Righteousness, which blesses and guides me,

to those who are of a better mind.

YASNA 60

PRAYERS FOR THE DWELLING PLACE

OF THE SACRIFICER

1. May your worthy servant and good citizen, O Great beneficent Lord, draw near to the better even more than to the good. Only You can show us the right way to journey through life, and how to nourish the physical, mental, and spiritual, in the holy everlasting realm where you dwell, O Ahura!

2. Let these blessings come to this house, these which are the wise perceptions of the saints, the sacred blessings granted to us through the ritual, with their guileless characteristics, together with their recognition

of what is due; and may the Righteous Order appear to us, and the Divine Sovereign Power, together with that which benefits us and grant us glorious welfare.

3. We ask this with the long enduring eminence of this Religion of Ahura's, the Zarathustrian Faith. And may all creation, and those of us dwelling here, be most quickly rewarded sanctity now with great speed, the strength of the holy, and Ahura's knowledge.

4. And may the good, heroic, and bountiful guardian spirits of the Fravashi come to us, and may they walk hand in hand with us with the healing virtues of the blessed gifts they grant us, as widespread as the earth, as far as

the rivers, as high as the sun, for the further improvement of all better people, for protection from the hostile, and for the abundance of riches and of glory.

5. May Obedience, whom we have named Sraosha, conquer disobedience within this dwelling, and may peace triumph over all disharmony in this house, and may generous giving triumph over greed, reverence over defiance, and truthful speech over dishonesty. May the Righteous Order conquer the Demon of Lies.

6. In this home, the Bountiful Immortal Souls implore us to carry out right worship of your holy words and to utter good praises of blessed

Obedience, who governs here. Indeed, the Immortal Souls implore us to make good sacrifice and acts of homage as a good offering to them for our salvation, and for a good offering in praise, as well as for the enduring, persevering offering of our entire selves.

7. We beg you not to let their brilliant glory to desert this house ever, nor the bright abundance they shine upon us. And never may they desert our children, nor our children's children. Any may they grant us that enduring, sustained companionship which brings us the continuance of that good blessedness which teaches us how to glorify you.

8. O Ahura Mazda, reign at Your will, and with a saving rule over all of Your own creatures, and grant to all holy people their own autonomous will over the waters, and over plants, and over all the clean and sacred beings which spring forth from Righteousness. And take away power from the wicked!

9. Let the holy be absolute in power, free from the control of wickedness! Cast out the enemy with the power of the creatures of Your Holy Spirit, which we call Spenta Mainyu, and may our enemies be conquered and rendered powerless over us.

10. I will encourage the heads of the houses, towns, and communities in whom Zarathustra

dwells, to the careful following of this Religion, which is that of Ahura and according to Zarathustra, in their thoughts, their words, and their actions.

11. Let our minds be enlightened, and our souls the best, and let our bodies be glorified. And let them, O Mazda, go likewise to the eternal realm as the best world of the saints as devoted to Ahura.

12. And let them be accompanied by Righteousness, whom we call Asha Vahishta, the most beautiful! And may we see You, and may we, approaching your realm, come near You, and grant us companionship with You. And we sacrifice to the Righteous Order, the

best, the most beautiful, the Bountiful Immortal

Soul!

YASNA 62

TO THE FIRE

1. I offer my praise and sacrifice to you, the Fire, the child of Ahura Mazda, as a good offering, an offering with the knowledge of our salvation, an offering of praise with benediction to you. You are worthy of sacrifice, and worthy of praise. And since you are worthy of sacrifice and praise, may you dwell in the hearts and homes of those who worship Mazda. Bring salvation to all who worship you in sincerity and truth, and enable us to keep the Fire burning.

2. And we shall always tend to you to keep you burning. Perpetually may you burn as we tend to you, to enjoy your brilliance and aroma. Let us nourish you so that you may burn brightly in our homes and within us, O Fire, child of Ahura Mazda!

3. Be alight within this house and burn brightly; shine and cast light upon all within this house. Burn perpetually to aid in the good heroism of renovation and progress, even past the millennium when your renovation will have been completed.

4. Grant me glory, nourishment, good thoughts, good speech, and a good mind for understanding others, O Fire, child of Ahura

Mazda. And may you grant me an expansive understanding that gains wisdom and power, that remains steadfast and constantly endures.

5. Grant me an understanding that is sure, alert, and true, that rises quickly when called upon, that likewise is helpful to others, to nurture them, to aid them, to draw them together, to influence them with Your word, grown to power, skillful, redeeming others from oppression, and served by many followers, which benefit my entire family, my town, and my community, which will endow the community with firm and righteous rulers.

6. Grant me wise instructors, O Fire, child of Ahura Mazda, whose wisdom both now and

eternally, with the divine light of Heaven and the best life of the saints, will shine brilliant and forever glorious. And let me have a good reward, good reputation, and a patient, prepared soul.

7. The Fire of Ahura Mazda brings this admonition to all to nourish them. From all these things, the Fire wishes to secure good and healthful care for us, the care of a true praiser, guarding our salvation.

8. At the hands of all who come by the Fire, it looks keenly upon them. What brings these soul-mates together, those who walk alone or sit at home? We worship, you O bounteous Fire.

9. And if a person who passes brings wood to the Fire, brought with good measure and with sacred care, or if a person brings the Baresman, representing our sacred plants, and spreads it with sanctity, or brings other offerings, then afterwards Ahura Mazda's Fire will bless them, contented, not offended, and satisfied.

10. Ahura will say unto you: Let the joy of all creation be with you, and a multitude with like, active minds go with you, and with active souls as well. You shall live your life, your days and nights, with a blessed soul. This is the blessing of the Fire for those who bring it well-dried wood, perfect for a brilliant flame, and purified

with the sincere blessing of the sacred ritual truth.

11. We strive after the flowing of the good waters, and their ebb as well, and the sound of their waves, desiring their absolution; I desire to approach them with my praise.

KHORDA AVESTA 6

Hymn to the Sun

Khwarshed Yasht

May Ahura Mazda be rejoiced! Holiness is the best of all good! I confess myself a worshipper of Mazda, a follower of Zarathustra, one who hates the evil of the spirits that we call the Daevas and obeys the laws of Ahura. For sacrifice, prayer, redemption, and glorification unto the holy and overseer of holiness; unto the shining, brilliant, eternal Sun; let there be redemption, with sacrifice, prayer, and glory. The will of the Ahura is the law of holiness.

1. We sacrifice unto the shining, brilliant, eternal Sun. When the light of the Sun becomes warmer, when the brightness of the Sun becomes warmer, then the heavenly divinities and angels will stand up by hundreds and thousands. They will gather together the Glory of the Sun; they will make its Glory pass down, they will pour its Glory upon the earth, made by Ahura; for the abundance of the world of holiness, for the abundance of the creatures of holiness, for the abundance of the shining, brilliant, eternal Sun.

2. And when the sun rises up, then the earth, made by Ahura, becomes clean; the running waters become clean, the waters of the wells

become clean, the waters of the sea become clean, the still waters become clean; and all the holy creatures, those creatures of the Good Spirit, become clean.

3. If the Sun should not rise up, then the evil Daevas would destroy all the things that are in the seven divisions of the earth, nor would the heavenly divinities and angels find any way of withstanding or repelling them here in the material world.

4. Those who offer up a sacrifice unto the shining, brilliant, eternal Sun – to withstand darkness, to withstand the Daevas born of darkness, to withstand wrong-doers and

criminals, to withstand the demonic beings, to withstand death that creeps in unseen – offer their sacrifice up to Ahura Mazda, to the archangels, and to their own souls. They rejoice with all the heavenly and worldly divinities and angels, who offer up a sacrifice unto the shining, brilliant, eternal Sun.

5. I will sacrifice unto Mithra, the ruler of wide pastures, who has a thousand ears and ten thousand eyes. I will sacrifice unto the club of Mithra, the ruler of wide pastures, well struck down upon the evil Daevas. I will sacrifice unto that friendship, the best of all friendships, that reigns between the moon and the sun.

6. For its brightness and glory, I will offer unto it a sacrifice worthy of being heard, namely, unto the shining, brilliant, eternal Sun. Unto the shining, brilliant, eternal Sun, we offer up the drinks, divine plants, meat, Baresman, kindling for the Fire, the wisdom of the tongue, the holy acts, the speech, the deeds, and the rightly-spoken words. Ahura Mazda, the Wise God, knows better than anyone those people who worship and make glorious sacrifices. We, for our part, honor all such people.

7. The will of the Ahura is the law of holiness. I bless the sacrifice and the command, and the strength and vigor of the shining, brilliant, eternal Sun. Holiness is the best of all good.

Give unto us brightness and glory, give us healthy bodies, give us the bright, all-happy, blissful abode of the holy Ones.

VISPERAD

Extensions to the liturgy

VISPERAD 15 – OBEDIENCE

1. Prepare your feet in readiness, and your hands, and your understanding, for doing good deeds well, in accordance with the sacred Order, all you Zarathustrian Mazdayasnians! Likewise, prepare to shun the unlawful and evil deeds which are contrary to our rituals and beliefs. Let all good deeds be done and give wealth to the needy.

2. Let Obedience, whom we call by the name Sraosha, be present here for the worship of Ahura Mazda, the most helpful and holy, who

is so desired by us in our utterances and service, and in our pondering of the Worship in Seven Hymns, and the heart's devotion to them, for their memorization and victorious and holy recitation, with nothing added and nothing left out.

3. It has been intoned, and shall be uttered as great, powerful, and conquering in victory, without harmful malice, for our expression of victorious words for Ahura Mazda's Fire.

4. We offer homage and sacrifices in this praise of Mazda, of the Immortal Souls, and of the divine Ahura on high, to show appreciation for the sacrifices that have accomplished

Mazda's goals for us, and which is in praise of the blessedness that has come to us, and of that well-timed prayer for blessings offered in the ritual.

5. This is likewise the praise of the bounteous word of reason, which we call Mathra Spenta, and of the Mazdayasnian Religion, and the praises of our scriptures, the Yasnas, which is also that of all the lords of the ritual, and of all the well-timed prayers for blessings, sacrifice, homage, redemption, and glorification of the entire creation of the holy and the clean.

VISPERAD 16

WORSHIP

1. And we worship the Fire, the child of Ahura Mazda, and the Rashnus, the divine beings of judgment who have the foundation of fire in them, and we worship the Fravashis, the protective guardian spirits of the saints. And we worship Obedience, who obtains the victory, and the holy people, and the entire creation of the holy and the clean.

2. And we worship the blessedness and the Fravashi of Zarathustra Spitama, the saint and protective guardian spirit of Zarathustra. And we worship all the saints and their blessed protective guardian spirits in communion. And

we worship their protective guardian spirits individually, and those of the saints within our community, and those of the saints outside our community, as we worship the protective guardian spirits of all holy people devoted to the Order of the Faith, wherever they may be. And we sacrifice to those whose service for us in the Yasna Ahura Mazda, the holy, known as the better, and of these Zarathustra is the living ruler and leader. And we sacrifice to the fields and the waters, the lands and the plants, and to the constituent parts of our Worship in Seven Hymns, its chapters, its metered lines, its, syntax, and its words.

Made in the USA
Columbia, SC
19 September 2024

42672203R00062